DOGS THROUGHOUT HISTORY™

The Story of the Dachshund

Jennifer Quasha

The Rosen Publishing Group's
PowerKids Press™
New York

For Casper and Corky

Published in 2000 by The Rosen Publishing Group, Inc.
29 East 21st Street, New York, NY 10010

First Edition

Book design: Danielle Primiceri

Photo credits: Cover, pp. 4, 19 © Robert Pearcy/Animals Animals; p. 7 © CORBIS/Roger Wood; p. 8 © CORBIS/National Gallery Collection; p. 11 © CORBIS/Dewitt Jones; p. 12 © CORBIS/o. Alamany & E. Vicens; p. 15 © CORBIS/Yann Arthus-Bertrand; p. 16 © Ralph Reinhold/Animals Animals and CORBIS/Reinhard Eisele; p. 20 CORBIS-Hulton-Deutsch Collection.

Quasha, Jennifer.
     The story of the dachshund / by Jennifer Quasha.
          p.   cm.—(Dogs throughout history)
     Includes index.
     Summary: Discusses the physical characteristics, history, and uses of the dachshund, a breed first used as a hunting dog to catch badgers.
     ISBN 0-8239-5516-8 (lib. bdg. : alk. paper)
     1. Dachshunds—History—Juvenile literature. 2 Dachshunds—Juvenile literature. [1. Dachshunds. 2. Dogs.] I. Title. II. Series.
SF429.D25Q36 1999
636.753'8—dc21   99-11606
                                                                                        CIP
                                                                                        AC

Manufactured in the United States of America

Contents

1   The Dachshund   5

2   The Earliest Dachshunds   6

3   Saint Hubert Dogs   9

4   Badger Dogs   10

5   Dachshunds in England   13

6   Dachshunds Come to America   14

7   The Ugly Dachshund   17

8   Daring Dachshunds   18

9   Budge, the Dachshund   21

10   Dachshunds Today   22

      Web Sites   22

      Glossary   23

      Index   24

The Dachshund

Dachshunds are sometimes called "sausage dogs" because they are long and skinny, like a sausage or hot dog. Dachshunds have very short legs, but walk proudly with their heads held high. They can have one of three different kinds of **coats**: shorthair, wire hair, or longhair. All Dachshunds are **bred** in two sizes: standard and miniature. Standard Dachshunds are bigger than Miniature Dachshunds. Standard Dachshunds are ten inches high. Miniature Dachshunds are just six inches high. People believe that the short-haired Dachshund is the oldest type of Dachshund. This is because paintings of dogs that look like short-haired Dachshunds have been found on old Egyptian **tombs**.

◄ *These Dachshund puppies will grow to weigh around eleven pounds.*

5

The Earliest Dachshunds

A relative of the Dachshund lived in Egypt 4,000 years ago. These dogs were called Teckels. Teckels were long, skinny dogs with short legs, just like Dachshunds. People know this because there are Egyptian tombs and **monuments** that have pictures of these dogs on them. There are also wall paintings that show pictures of these ancient Dachshund relatives. Around 1900 B.C., a **pharaoh** named Sesostris kept dogs like Dachshunds that helped him hunt badgers, foxes, and other small animals.

The Egyptian pharaoh, Sesostris, loved Dachshund-like dogs called Teckels. ▶

Saint Hubert Dogs

   Many Dachshund lovers think that Dachshunds are related to dogs called Saint Hubert dogs. This is because Dachshunds look very similar to Saint Hubert dogs. Like Dachshunds, these dogs were long and thin, and had short legs. Saint Hubert dogs lived in the 1500s in a country called Belgium. They got this name because they lived at the Saint Hubert **monastery**. The monks who lived in the monastery kept these helpful dogs to hunt badgers, rabbits, and foxes.

◀ *This picture of Saint Hubert shows that he loved animals, especially dogs.*

Badger Dogs

Dachshunds have lived for many hundreds of years in a country called Germany. In the German language, the word *dachs* means badger, and *hund* means hound or dog. The word Dachshund means badger hound, or badger dog. Dachshunds were first used as hunting dogs to catch badgers. A badger is a small animal that lives underground. The Dachshund would go down a small hole in the ground and catch the badgers who lived there. Dachshunds were very good at this job because of their long, lean bodies.

Badgers weigh between 25 and 40 pounds. ▶

Dachshunds in England

The popularity of Dachshunds as pets slowly began to spread throughout Europe in the 1800s. In 1845, Prince Albert bought an **adorable** Dachshund for his wife, Queen Victoria. At the time, Queen Victoria was the young queen of England. She became queen when she was only eighteen years old. She ruled over England for more than 60 years before she died in 1901. Queen Victoria named her Dachshund "Dash." Sometimes the queen would dress Dash in a red jacket and trousers. The attention she gave Dash helped to make Dachshunds a favorite pet among English people.

◀ *Queen Victoria of England loved Dachshunds.*

13

Dachshunds Come to America

Dachshunds in America today are **descendants** of the Dachshunds that came from Germany. These Dachshunds began coming to America in the late 1870s. Many Dachshunds were brought to America by German travelers who came to visit the United States. Some German people moved to America permanently and brought their pet Dachshunds with them. Dachshunds also came to America with soldiers in the U.S. military. The soldiers brought Dachshunds home from Germany after World War I and World War II. By the early 1940s, Dachshunds had become one of the ten most popular dogs in America.

Dachshunds are long and skinny and fun to hug. ▶

The Ugly Dachshund

In 1938, an author named G. B. Stern wrote a book called *The Ugly Dachshund*. It is about a Great Dane puppy who lives with a family of Dachshunds. The Great Dane thinks he's a Dachshund, too, but an ugly one. He even tries to act just like a Dachshund, but he has trouble because he is a much bigger dog. The Great Dane feels sad because he is different from his family. Then he realizes he can do things that Dachshunds can't do, like run fast and see over high walls. The Great Dane learns that he is special in his own way. This story helped to make Dachshunds even more popular and loved throughout America.

◄ *The story of* The Ugly Dachshund *was made into a movie in 1965.*

Daring Dachshunds

Dachshunds are known to be very brave dogs. They are not afraid to chase animals that are bigger than they are. This is because they were bred to hunt badgers, and badgers are about as big as Dachshunds. Being badger dogs also trained Dachshunds to be **persistent**. Once a Dachshund starts to chase something, there's not much that can stop her. Dachshunds were trained to catch the badgers no matter how long it took. Patient Dachshunds would wait until they caught the badger, even if they were tired and had been waiting a long time.

This wire-haired Dachshund is patiently waiting to catch a badger. ▶

Budge, the Dachshund

Since Dachshunds are so long and skinny, they sometimes have problems with their backs. Budge is a very brave and **courageous** Dachshund. Budge is a Dachshund whose back legs are **paralyzed**. Fortunately, Budge's owners found something to help him. They bought him a cart that attaches to his back legs. The cart has wheels that Budge can pull with his front legs. Now Budge can move on his own again. Budge loves to chase things and play ball. His favorite game is fetch. Even though Budge has a **disability**, he still likes to have fun with his family.

◀ *Dachshunds often have bad back problems because they are so long and thin. This Dachshund, like Budge, is a very brave dog.*

Dachshunds Today

Today, Dachshunds are very popular dogs throughout the world. Dachshunds are still sometimes used for hunting in countries like England, Germany, and Switzerland. In the United States, however, most Dachshunds are kept as wonderful pets. People love to have them around because they are friendly, cheerful dogs. Dachshunds like to exercise and play. Although they are little, these dogs have a big bark. They are very **alert** and make good watchdogs, too. Dachshunds are spirited and loving, and they make caring companions for people.

Web Sites

http://www.goldendox.com/tdn/dox.htm

http://www.clinet.fi/~zone/rikusivut/koirat2.html

Glossary

adorable (uh-DOR-uh-bul) Cute and delightful.

alert (uh-LERT) Paying attention to what is going on around you.

bred (BREHD) A male and female animal that have been brought together so that they can have babies.

coat (COHT) An animal's fur.

courageous (kuh-RAY-jus) To be brave or to have strength that comes from inside.

descendants (dih-SEN-dents) People or animals born of a certain family or group.

disability (dis-uh-BIL-ih-tee) A difference in someone's body that makes him or her unable to do certain things the same way others can.

monastery (MAH-nuh-stair-ee) A religious building where monks live, work, and worship together.

monument (MAHN-yu-mint) Something set up to honor a person or an event.

paralyzed (PAR-uh-lized) When you can't feel or move all or part of your body.

persistent (per-SIS-tint) To keep trying, to refuse to stop.

pharaoh (FAYR-oh) Name given to ancient Egyptian kings.

tomb (TOOM) A grave or vault for a dead body, often above ground.

Index

A
adorable, 13
alert, 22

B
bred, 5, 18
Budge, 21

C
coats, 5
courageous, 21

D
Dash, 13
descendants, 14
disabilities, 21

H
hunting badgers, 6, 9, 10, 18

M
monasteries, 9
monuments, 6

P
paralyzed, 21
patience, 18
persistent, 18
pharaohs, 6
popularity, 13, 14, 17, 22
Prince Albert, 13

Q
Queen Victoria, 13

S
Saint Hubert dogs, 9
Sesostris, 6
Stern, G. B., 17

T
Teckels, 6
tombs, 5

U
Ugly Dachshund, The, 17

W
World Wars, 14